The Goddess Chronicals

Angela Holmes

BookLeaf Publishing

India | USA | UK

Presentation by *BookLeaf Publishing*

Web: www.bookleafpub.com

E-mail: info@bookleafpub.com

ISBN: 9789358314786

First edition 2024

To all who are wondering and feel lost, to all the Goddesses and Gods who love deep and sacrifice the Self. You are your ultimate love

ACKNOWLEDGEMENT

I acknowledge all of the Divine love lessons that helped me see myself as the ultimate guide, lover, and master of myself.

PREFACE

I was able to see the growth through the pain
and recovery of love of others to a self
realization of the love within and expressed to
self. Writing these words created an awakening
and a vivid realization of growth and the
Owerful magic of words. Knowing now that
words are spells. I evolved into using the power
of a hopeless romantic and transmuting those
energies to manifest the life and love I've always
possessed within. The Divine Self

Love!

Love!

I used to run from you
Now I run to you

Love!

I used to despise
Love
I'd try to disguise
Love

But now I feel baptized
By love
Hypnotized
Mesmerized

And all I do is fanatisize
About you

Love!

Love! Revalued

Was never too shy for
Love!

Would always ride or die for
Love!

Never hesitated to gamble put my heart on the
line
Flipped it like a dime for you
Love!

Pimped it and pandered it
Slummed it and slandered it
Then flipped it and scripted it
Was the driver and the shooter for you
Love!

I realized my gift
Instead of seeking outside of my Self for you
Love!

I now focus on my Love from within

Stopped chasin that which was worthless
Those who treated me as if I was worth less

While all the while within me
God's kingdom dwells

Love!

Letting go of the past drama
Only seeing the lessons
Since the knowledge and wisdom
I meditate on I now receive
My richness within

Much gratitude for teaching me
Love!

As I chased Love I was led to the power that
dwells within

Love!

NO LONGER DO I FANTASIZE I AM NOT
HYPNOTIZED OR MESMERIZED
THE GREATEST LOVE IS THE LOVE FOR
YOURSELF

know thyself

LOVE!

Confusion

When can I say?
When will I see?
How long must it take,
Until the answer comes to me?

Where have we been?
What have we gone through?
Is there an answer?
Or, do I expect too much from you?

Is it taking too long?
Am I wasting my time?
Or am I just impatient?
Are these games you're playing with my mind?

Am I the only one confused?
Or does this situation amuse you?
Are these questions too much?

Are you turned on by how I pursue you?
Sometimes I want to give up
But I can't imagine my life without you

I do not feel I should beg
And you cannot stand when I harass you

Am I the piece to your puzzle that does not
actually fit?
Can you not tell I'm getting sick of this shit?

So when you finally wake up
And come to a conclusion
Call 911 because I'm drowning in confusion

Drug

When Love is your drug of choice

I refuse to be held captive

By fake kisses
And temporary lusts

Keep that shit for the hopeless

I am a woman full of faith
I am fearless

I can wait for the truth
I'm addicted to
Love

Abuse

Been beaten with sticks and stones
Yet still I stand

Although it is hard to stay strong when weak
women are in demand

Men are ashamed to show their faces
Because empty are their hands

Little do they know
Knowledge and wisdom are priceless
And what we need to know is real men do exist

And always love is the answer
I have seen enough fists

The Ambiguous Ex

I sit consciously trying to prepare
For the next transition in my journey
As subconsciously keeping my focus on the
vision before me
Although I pursue my faith
I am holding on to a past love
I know I am not in a psychotic delusion
When I tell you he still possesses the deep flesh
of my heart

I am in the process of repairing an aching spirit
Once passionate and eager to explore the depths

Now I am timid with no interest to explore

I'm still holding on to your whispers in my ear
The flattering words
The compliments
The constant affection
You once showered me with love

This Pisces Goddess still feels the connection
To her Scorpion King

I am still grieving for your abscence I cry
constantly
Your return is a necessity

Although I anticipate your return
I'm desparate for your touch

Come home!

We have a forth chakra spiritual connection
Not many can add kind of connections
Because they let fear interfere

You should never let fear come between you and
love

I desire you my cowardish love
Disloyal love
Selfish love
Let my spirit go!
If you are going to let fear keep you away

Love always

The Ambiguous Ex

Continued

The way your breath made my skin tingle as you
Whispered sweet nothings in my ear

Those electrical currents of energy
The law of magnetism at its finest

You got your freedom
To the memory of your love I'm enslaved

I saw within you divinity
And for some odd reason you ran from mine

You were not
Ready for the throne

Now I'm alone on my throne
Scarred to the bone
By a love unworthy of my shine
He can't hang with my grind

You are unaware of the sorrow
Holding on to the faded traces of your footprints

Unsure if I even want you to return

A cold wind blows

It was the summer heat

You blew in like a breath of fresh air

I'm hot your hot
We were the perfect pair

Through the heat through the lust even the sin
You blew my mind and raised my spirit
Kissed my soul

I still feel you in my skin

But as soon as the seasons changed you flew out
With the wind

Although October was 31 days of non stop
satisfaction

He waited for the coldest day to get distracted

As a cold wind blows
You left me with chills
You left me with withdrawals
As if addicted to pain pills

As a cold wind blows
And skies are gray
It was that spring storm in April
And here it is the last day of May

Every time the Sun kisses my skin I feel you
I still feel your heat
as a cold wind blows
Strong and indiscreet

I still feel the chill
But crave your summer heat

Insanity

Insanity insanity
No longer do I live insanitly
All praise to the GODDESS
I now realize my validity
My dreams are now reality
With a heart filled with solidity
I honor my creativity
I recongnize the Goddess that dwells with in me
I represent
Exquisitely
Divinity
Femininity
Plus brilliancy

My beliefs are infinity

Mastermind

Only you can Master your mind

You are the master of your mind

Be mindful of what you allow in

Be mindful of your self talk
Always be kind to you

Master your words
Words are spells
Cast by you

Master your mind
You are magic

Master your self
Master of self

Mastermind it is Universal

The Self

As I sit in silence
I let all thoughts and feelings subside
Although I am grateful for the body and the
mind
I know that I am the core substance,
I am the Self
The soul of my existence
The past, the present and the future of the All
It all begins and resides within
The Self

I am telling you the only way to execute this self
study and evaluation is to be alone sit in silence
With the Self
Go within, tap in, and listen and see what
thoughts and feelings arise for you

Do not seek yourself outside of yourself

Many seek theirselves through materials and
vices and self infliction

Our relationship with Self is vital and our most
important relationship we will ever encounter

So take time to acknowledge and appreciate
The Self

Self Love

I vibrate high

I vibrate high
My soul is glow

I vibrate high
I elevate my energies when low

I raise my vibration my frequencies flow
Into higher realities realms and dimensions

I vibrate high
This is my ascension

Enlightenment my thoughts
I visualize and expand
My reality shifts
Immediately at my command

I vibrate high

Moksha

I am in the frequency of my highest Self
I stay in this frequency by turning my energy
inward

My intuition is aligned
Better said I am aligned with my intuition
The Self has all of the answers
Ask and listen

Breath
Inhale
Hold
Exhale

Chant
I Release all delusions from my mind
I release all delusions from my mind

I release all illusions I realease all illusion
I realease all illusions from my mind

Birth death and rebirth

Free yourself from the bondage of your mind

Moksha

The P's

Praying Prisoners Paying Prophets Preachers
Pasters Pimping Pedophile Priests
Popping Pills Paying Prostitutes Puberty
Policing Politic Perverts Party Panties Pink
Panther Power Priveledge Peace

Poetic

Pathetic People Paying Preachers Pasters Police
Politicians Priests
Pimping Pandering Pedophelia Prostitutes
Popping Pills Pink Panties Peace Pipes
Perverted Pesticides Peculiar Penalties Persist
Pistols Packing Priveledge Plausible Plauge
Paranoid Parasites Protests Prisoners
Pandamonium
Prophets
Poets
Peep

I Am Protected

I am Protected

I am tuned in to all of my ancestors that were
tuned in and protected

I call in protection over my children's children's
children

I am calling in wealth for myself and my
families famillies family

I am knowledge wisdom wealth health and
power

I speak power into myself and all who reside
near and who
I come in contact with

I am casting spells of abundance mental
wellness health wealth power abundance

I Am

Reminder

I am poetic like Pac
prolific like Nip
Writing in this notebook
Keeping journals like
Thoth

Meditation as I chant
manifesting as I visualize
Exactly what I want

I affirm my reality
I reject all that is not meant
As I vibrate on the frequencies
As I elevate to dimensions of enlightenment

I continue to shine
I continue to be Devine

The Matrix

It's pretty much mind tricks
The system created
That keeps us living in a loop

Everything that is outside of yourself
That leaves you confused and trapped

You will Not find the Matrix on a map
It is everywhere and no where at all
At the same time

To get out of the matrix you have to take back
control of your mind

Eliminate the invisible chains that keep you in
bind

Emancipate yourselves you control your own
mind

Money and materials are all part of the plan

They keep you bound to the matrix,
The ultimate middle man

To escape the matrix you have to elevate from
the Third dimension

To escape the matrix is a spiritual
Ascension

Raise your vibration
Evolve your destiny
Escaping the matrix is leaving the slave
Mentality behind you
Let it all go
This also includes your ego,
Eliminate delusions
And frequencies that are low

Keep your head on a swivel
Don't be a slave to the trap
Don't be a slave to the system
Be sovereign and independent
It's the only resolution

Escaping the matrix is a spiritual revolution

Universal mind

I am Divine
Vibrating in my own
Time space

I opened the portals of my soul
I remove all illusions from my
Mind space

My intuition is no longer ignored
I am no longer ignorant
A realization of self,
Self discovery with vigilance

I keep taking deep breaths
And inhaling incense

I chant words of affirmation
I recognize my higher self

My energies high
Elevated
There is only one mind
I am I tuned with it

We all are one

Spells

25

I am casting vibrant spells
With my beautiful words that radiate my
existence

I affirm over my life that
I lack nothing
I overflow with prosperity
And abundance

Love fills me
Rather I am full of love

I feel euphoric
This frequency fills my life

My visions are so vivid I see me full
My visions are so vivid I feel it I see it

These words are spells being positively casted
I cast spells with words writing spells being
casted

Nature

I am vibrating with the frequency of nature
Infinite power flowing to me and through me

I am abundant vibrant, with
Wisdom and knowledge
Ever increasing always learning about
The Self

The life long journey of moksha
Illuminating the delusions of my mind

Vibrating in the frequency of bliss and
understanding

Nature

Sovereign

27

I am sovereign
I own myself and my time
I chose what I do
No one controls me

I am free from mental delusions
Nothing bounds me
Freedom
Freedom
Freedom

I am free

Seeker of the Self
Only you can free yourself